RAND NATIONAL DEFENSE RESEARCH

T0108971

The Role of Logic Modeling in a Collaborative and Iterative Research Process

Lessons from Research and Analysis Conducted with the Federal Voting Assistance Program

Victoria A. Greenfield, Shoshana R. Shelton,
Edward Balkovich

Prepared for the Office of the Secretary of Defense

For more information on this publication, visit www.rand.org/t/RR882z1

Library of Congress Cataloging-in-Publication Data is available for this publication.
ISBN: 978-0-8330-9297-7

Limited Print and Electronic Distribution Rights

The RAND Corporation is a research organization that develops solutions to public policy challenges to help make communities throughout the world safer and more secure, healthier and more prosperous. RAND is nonprofit, nonpartisan, and committed to the public interest.

RAND's publications do not necessarily reflect the opinions of its research clients and sponsors.

Support RAND
Make a tax-deductible charitable contribution at
www.rand.org/giving/contribute

www.rand.org

Preface

In early 2013, the leadership of the Federal Voting Assistance Program (FVAP) commissioned the RAND National Defense Research Institute to undertake a collaborative, multiyear project known formally as FVAP and the Road Ahead. The project was established to assist FVAP in aligning its strategy and operations to better serve its mission and stakeholders and to strengthen FVAP's capacity to set its own course, embrace change, and communicate its role in the voting community.

Through an evidence-based approach founded in logic modeling, the RAND project team worked with FVAP to compare, reconcile, and align what was in the agency's strategy and typical of its operations and what should be. The team delivered recommendations and implementing guidance over the course of the project, and FVAP enacted change throughout.

This report focuses on the collaborative development and application of the logic model. It describes the underlying method and frames the approach in generalizable, step-by-step terms, drawing examples from the project with FVAP. The report derives from a more detailed report that more fully documents both the process and its results, including recommendations, guidance, and organizational change.

This report should be of interest to agencies seeking to use logic models to improve their strategic and operational alignment and develop a better understanding of the methods and processes available to do so.

This research was sponsored by FVAP and conducted within the Forces and Resources Policy Center and the Acquisition Technology Policy Center of the RAND National Defense Research Institute, a federally funded research and development center sponsored by the Office of the Secretary of Defense, the Joint Staff, the Unified Combatant Commands, the Navy, the Marine Corps, the defense agencies, and the defense Intelligence Community.

For more information on the RAND Forces and Resources Policy Center, see www.rand.org/nsrd/ndri/centers/frp or contact the director. For more information on the RAND Acquisition and Technology Policy Center, see www.rand.org/nsrd/ndri/centers/atp or contact the director. Contact information for each director is provided on each program's web page.

Contents

Figures and Table

Figures

Tables

Acknowledgments

We thank the leadership and staff of the Federal Voting Assistance Program. They gave us their time, energy, and trust over a period of many months as we sought to deepen our understanding of their organization and its role in voting assistance and, in so doing, to learn about the unique circumstances of absentee voting for uniformed-service members and their families and for U.S. citizens residing overseas. We are also grateful to Leonard William Braverman and Frank Camm, both of the RAND Corporation, and to Harry P. Hatry of the Urban Institute for their formal reviews of the companion report, *The Federal Voting Assistance Program and the Road Ahead: Achieving Institutional Change Through Analysis and Collaboration* (Greenfield, Shelton, et al., 2015). We also thank the many people, including congressional staff, voting assistance officers and office managers, state and local election officials, representatives of overseas-citizen groups, academics and technologists, and election advocates who shared their perspectives on voting assistance over the course of the project. Lastly, we thank Michelle Horner for her patient and careful support in preparing this document for publication and Lisa Bernard for a thoughtful and thorough edit.

Abbreviations

ADM	active-duty military
CSG	Council of State Governments
CVAO	chief Voting Assistance Officer
DHRA	Defense Human Resources Activity
DMDC	Defense Manpower Data Center
DoD	U.S. Department of Defense
DoDD	Department of Defense directive
DoDI	Department of Defense instruction
DOJ	U.S. Department of Justice
DOS	U.S. Department of State
DTIC	Defense Technical Information Center
EAC	U.S. Election Assistance Commission
ETS	Electronic Transmission Service
FPCA	Federal Post Card Application
FVAP	Federal Voting Assistance Program
FWAB	Federal Write-In Absentee Ballot
GAO	U.S. Government Accountability Office
GSA	General Services Administration
HR	human resources
IG	inspector general

pantry or warehouse, the people who need the food might constitute its final customers; they are the ultimate targets of the organization's efforts. Intermediate customers might include organizations that share a link to online information about the pantry or warehouse or organizations that prepare and deliver food for consumption. Application and transformation, thus, can involve something as simple as alerting people to the existence of the food or as complex as meal preparation and delivery.

We sometimes refer to *intermediaries* more generally as the individuals or entities that an organization needs to reach its final customers and affect outcomes. They can be direct consumers of a program's outputs (i.e., intermediate customers) or partners. In the context of a food pantry, a partner might be a sister organization that collects food for the pantry or provides volunteer staffing. Note that the same individual or entity might, in some instances, serve as a partner and, in other instances, as an intermediate customer.

The path from inputs to outcomes might not be strictly linear. Feedback loops can play a part in operations. For example, an organization that prepares and delivers meals to final customers might, in the course of its efforts, gather information on needs within a community that serves as a planning input for the pantry or warehouse.

An organization's strategy consists of goals and objectives, as well as measures that the organization uses to determine whether its objectives and goals are being met. These goals and objectives are related to the inputs, activities, outputs, customer activities, and intended outcomes of an organization. On the input end, an organization, such as a nonprofit food pantry or warehouse, might seek to increase funding over a given period or to update its facilities. At the other end of the spectrum, strategic goals are associated with the outcomes that an organization wants to achieve. A food pantry or warehouse might, as noted previously, want to reach and meet the nutritional needs of an eligible population.

The logic-model template requires strict vertical alignment between strategy and operations. In other words, a program's strategy and operations should make sense as a package and "line up." As the vertical double arrows in Figure 2.1 indicate, strategic goals should relate to the program's contribution to outcomes, as in the case of nutritional sufficiency; intermediate goals should relate to customer activities, such as food delivery and consumption, which might involve changes in knowledge, attitudes, or behavior. Similarly, the performance measures that are posited for each stage should enable programs to gauge progress in meeting the corresponding goals and objectives. If the goal is to reach and meet the nutritional needs of an eligible population, a measure might involve reaching and serving a particular share of that population. The measure might increase over time as an organization gathers more funding or updates its facilities and improves its service delivery. The relationships among operations, goals, and measures should be direct, transparent, and supportable with evidence.

The red dotted line, positioned beneath customer activities, intermediate goals, and intermediate measures, signifies a point along the path at which a program's control greatly diminishes. An organization can expect to exercise a reasonable amount of control over how it uses inputs to produce outputs and how it transfers its outputs to its customers, but it can expect to have much less control after that transfer occurs. A food warehouse cannot, for example, control the ways in which another organization prepares or delivers meals.

The model also includes external factors that, by definition, are not under the organization's control but could affect its future operations. Changes in external factors, such as the enactment of a new requirement for an organization, a reduction in funding, or the emergence of a new technology, can affect the program's orientation and the extent to which it can achieve outcomes. For example, a food pantry or warehouse might need to restructure its operations in response to new storage or handling requirements. Having identified a set of relevant external factors, an organization might benefit from monitoring the factors and, if possible, planning for plausible changes in circumstances.

A primary strength of the template is the close integration of the operational and strategic domains, enabling it to serve multiple roles with a high degree of internal consistency:

- As a tool for fleshing out the relationships between inputs, activities, outputs, customers, and outcomes, the model can be used to better focus a program's operations—and direct its resources—to help fill a societal need or fix a societal problem.
- As a foundation for establishing a program's strategy, the model can be used to "walk back" from a program's overarching mission—its reason for existing—to formulate goals and objectives that speak to its operations.
- As a communication device, the model can be used to provide internal and external audiences, including program partners, legislators, and other stakeholders, with a clear representation of the program's operations and intent. The model can also be used to delineate a program's boundaries and responsibilities, thereby clarifying the meaning of *impact* and *results* as they relate to the program.
- As a framework for performance evaluation, it can also be used to select well-aligned measures, i.e., measures that closely line up with or correspond to a program's stated goals and objectives and, thus, provide an appropriate gauge of impact or results.

Example: Federal Voting Assistance Program Benchmark Logic Model

The numbers of inputs, activities, and outputs specified in a logic model and the relationships between them depend on the organization being modeled. The intent is to decompose and describe an organization's mission, strategy, and operations in terms that are meaningful to the organization as a whole, including its leadership and staff, and that can be communicated to others. Figure 2.2 shows an example of a completed, albeit partial, logic model: the FVAP benchmark logic model, which was a product of lengthy discussions with FVAP leadership and staff.

The benchmark logic model differs from the logic-model template in two important regards. First, the benchmark logic model begins and ends with a broad statement of FVAP's mission that is positioned at the top of the model—specifically, "To assist UOCAVA voters in voting successfully." Thus, the mission statement closes a loop between FVAP's inputs and end outcomes. Second, it does not explicitly render the flow of strategy from goals to objectives. In our work with FVAP, we treated FVAP's program design as indicative of its underlying strategy in the period of our analysis; thus, a close examination of the program's design and implementation provided insight to the agency's strategy and operations. Another RAND project was looking more closely at metrics and measures that could eventually support the development of a new strategic plan, but these features were outside the scope of our analysis. The remaining details of the model follow the general structure of the template, with only a few minor modifications, and include inputs, activities, outputs, partners and customers, intermediate outputs, intermediate outcomes, end outcomes, and external factors.

The left side of the diagram depicts three activity streams: voter assistance, election-official assistance, and institutional support, including communication and technical services. The contents of the activity boxes for voter and election-official assistance are quite similar. For example, both streams develop and modify training materials, guidance, and other online materials, as well as attend to relationships with customers and partners. What distinguishes the two streams is that the outputs are oriented toward different audiences. All three streams draw from the pool of FVAP's inputs, but each of them uses the inputs to produce distinct outputs. The two assistance streams, voter and election-official assistance, require institutional support from within FVAP to carry out their duties and, in turn, provide the organization with subject-matter expertise. For example, FVAP's communication staff could not be expected to develop the agency's message in reports, testimony, and other outlets without access to the ideas of other staff members with deep knowledge of voter and election-official assistance. The bottom of the bounding box of activities and outputs lists FVAP's partners.

The transfer step at the center of the diagram depicts how FVAP's outputs are conveyed to intermediate customers—such as the uniformed services, the U.S. Department of State, states and localities, nongovernmental organizations (NGOs), media outlets, and technologists and academics—and to end customers (namely, UOCAVA voters) through a variety of channels. Those channels include the FVAP website, bulk emails, conferences, hearings, and other person-to-person contact. The diagram shows the intermediate customers on which FVAP depends to serve its mission; the application and transformation of FVAP's outputs to create intermediate outputs, such as policies, plans, and research findings; and, both explicitly and implicitly, the flow of

Figure 2.2
Federal Voting Assistance Program Benchmark Logic Model

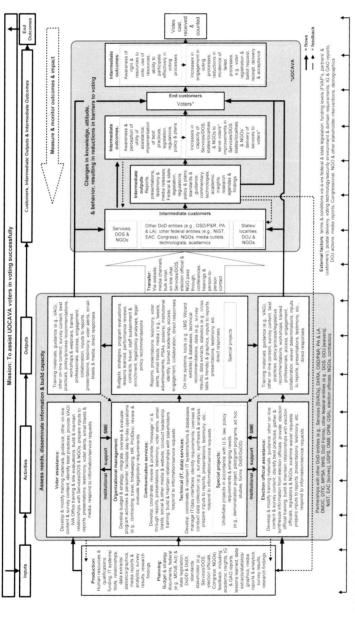

SOURCE: Greenfield, Shelton, et al., 2015.

NOTE: IT = information technology. MOVE = Military and Overseas Voter Empowerment. DoDD = DoD directive. DoDI = DoD instruction. DOS = U.S. Department of State. IG = inspector general. GAO = U.S. Government Accountability Office. SME = subject-matter expertise. HR = human resources. ProfDev = professional development. VAG = Voting Assistance Guide. PSA = public service announcement. LMS = learning management system. SVAO = Service Voting Action Officer. DHRA = Defense Human Resources Activity. OSD = Office of the Secretary of Defense. P&R = Under Secretary of Defense for Personnel and Readiness. PA = public affairs. LA = legislative affairs. DMDC = Defense Manpower Data Center. DTIC = Defense Technical Information Center. MPSA = Military Postal Service Agency. WHS = Washington Headquarters Service. DOJ = U.S. Department of Justice. EAC = U.S. Election Assistance Commission. USPS = U.S. Postal Service. OMB = Office of Management and Budget. OPM = Office of Personnel Management. GSA = General Services Administration.

information, expertise, and other resources that is needed to elicit intended end outcomes (specifically, "votes cast, received, and counted," at the far right of the diagram).

Some outputs constitute inputs to other activities that, in turn, give rise to additional outputs, both within and outside of FVAP. For example, academics might use FVAP's data to generate research findings that FVAP can then incorporate in its reports.

The arrows along the bottom of Figure 2.2 represent the external factors, such as federal and state legislation, funding, and voting technology, that could affect FVAP's operations.

The depiction in Figure 2.2 represents the agency's activity streams largely in accordance with its organizational structure (see Figure 2.3) and, on that basis, could be considered part logic model and part organizational chart.[4] This "hybridization" offered two benefits. First, it facilitated tracking the flow of similar activities and outputs, such as relationship-building and maintenance, which are directed at different audiences with potentially different needs. Second, it enabled us to draw out and highlight organizational concerns.

---

[4]   Greenfield, Williams, and Eiseman, 2006, discusses some of the different possible relationships between a logic model and organization's structure, indicating that that the two need not coincide.

Figure 2.3
Federal Voting Assistance Program Organization Chart as of April–May 2013

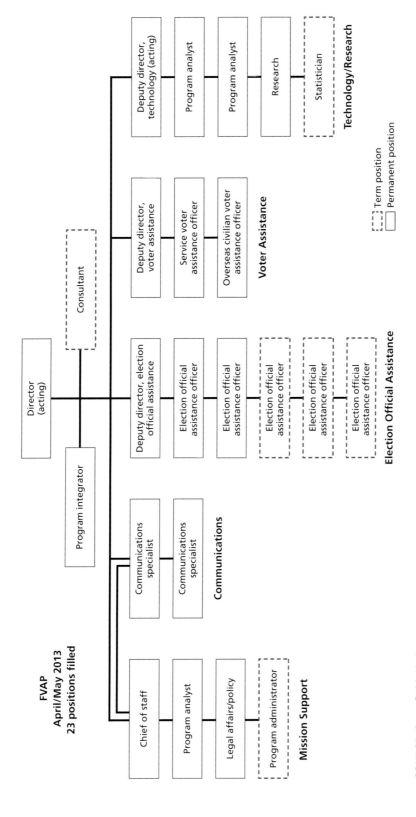

SOURCE: Greenfield, Shelton, et al., 2015.
NOTE: The line between Mission Support and Communications indicates that Communications, which had a direct line to the director, was also run as part of Mission Support. For some purposes, it was its own group; for others, it was part of Mission Support.

RAND RR882/1-2.3

CHAPTER THREE

A Collaborative Implementation of the Logic Model

A collaborative logic-modeling process requires trust between the logic modeler and the representatives of the program being modeled. Trust is needed so that all participants in the process, including the logic modeler and the program's leadership and staff, can access information about the program, are willing to share their views, and can withstand a critical examination of their points of view. Candid discussion of individual viewpoints can be important to understanding a program and reaching a common understanding of its mission, strategy, and operations. The extent to which a logic-modeling process is either collaborative or arm's length is a matter of degree. This project was highly collaborative, but there are other less collaborative ways to construct logic models that would have been more arm's length and required less FVAP involvement. RAND and other institutions have applied less collaborative methods in other projects.

Figure 3.1 depicts a general approach to applying the logic model in short-, medium-, and long-term projects that focus on the strategic and operational alignment of an organization.[1] Longer projects produce more-comprehensive results than shorter projects but begin similarly. The first step in the process is to develop the logic model with program leadership and staff to benchmark strategy and operations as the agency understands them. The next step is to test, validate, and refine the logic model, drawing from external perspectives, including, if possible, those of stakeholders. Then, the logic modeler works with the program to identify gaps and disconnects in the agency's program design and implementation and reconfirms leadership and staff perspectives as needed. The final step is to provide recommendations and guidance for realignment. The approach can be extended to meet the needs of a multiyear project by further probing for gaps and disconnects and then gathering evidence of change and realignment.

In this chapter, we describe the logic-modeling process that we used with FVAP, as depicted in the long-term path in Figure 3.1. In that case, the development of the benchmark logic model led us to identify gaps and disconnects in strategy and operations and to explore concerns about FVAP's research-related and military installation–

---

[1] For road maps of logic-model applications developed for other purposes, see, for example, Greenfield, Williams, and Eiseman, 2006; Landree, Miyake, and Greenfield, 2015; and Williams et al., 2009.

Figure 3.1
General Approach to Developing and Applying the Logic Model

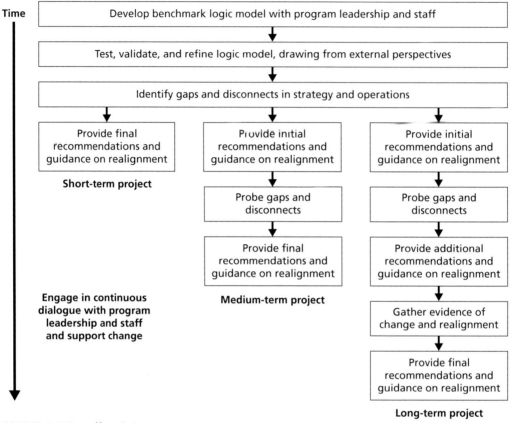

SOURCE: RAND staff analysis.
RAND RR882/1-3.1

based activities. We employed an auxiliary method, a system-wide analysis, to augment the logic-modeling results and provided additional recommendations for realignment, including recommendations specific to FVAP's research-related and military installation–based activities. We also gathered and weighed evidence of change within FVAP, some stemming from our collaborative efforts, including those on the logic model, and some emanating from FVAP, reflective of internally recognized needs.

The collaborative elements of the project were crucial to its success. Over the life of the project, we worked with FVAP in frequent face-to-face meetings to share, vet, and clarify ideas and to discuss and refine the details of our approach. The collaboration enabled us to develop a full, mutual understanding of FVAP's needs; to better gauge and adjust the tactics of our approach to meet those needs; and to rapidly transfer recommendations to FVAP leadership so that FVAP could implement change. The collaborative approach to logic modeling also gave FVAP a stake in both the process and the product and thus reinforced the agency's commitment to implementing change.

Although we describe the approach in terms of discrete steps in Figure 3.1, the elements of the approach are not neatly separable. For example, by the time we formally delivered our preliminary recommendations and guidance to FVAP, it had already begun to implement change. This was possible because we shared our findings as they emerged and worked in close communication with FVAP throughout the process.

Develop a Benchmark Logic Model

In the first step of the logic-modeling process, we worked with FVAP leadership and staff to learn about and document the agency's strategy and operations, including its organizational structure. We focused on identifying its inputs, activities, outputs, transfer mechanisms, partners, customers, and intended outcomes.[2] We also identified a substantial number of external factors, such as federal and state legislation, funding, and voting technology, that can affect the organization's strategy and operation.

The process involved both data collection and analysis. To provide context for our discussions with FVAP and to enhance our understanding of FVAP, we reviewed strategic documents, congressional testimony, training materials and guidance, surveys and reports, organizational charts, and governing legislation and policy.[3]

To begin developing FVAP's logic model, we held a two-day all-hands workshop with FVAP staff and leadership to explore the agency's mission, its operations, and, to a lesser extent, its strategy. Sessions introduced the use of logic modeling as a tool for better aligning program strategy and operations, including organizational structure, and for strengthening program communication. To spur the process, we provided FVAP staff and leadership with a set of discussion points, addressing three basic logic-modeling concepts—specifically, who are "you" as a program or program area, what are you doing, and why are you doing it—in advance of the workshop (see Appendix A). Typically, an agency's mission statement would serve as a foundation and an aim point for this type of logic model; however, an initial session of the workshop, titled, "Why Does FVAP Exist?" confirmed that FVAP staff members lacked a common, shared understanding of the organization's purpose. To fill the immediate need for a foundation, we proposed, discussed, and adopted a proxy mission statement, i.e., "to assist UOCAVA voters in voting successfully."

---

[2] As noted in Chapter Two, another closely related RAND project worked with FVAP on the development of metrics and measures.

[3] For this purpose, we did not closely examine the law or policy, as we did for the later discussion of core requirements; rather, we read it as a backdrop to our conversations with FVAP and the model-development process.

On the second day of the workshop, we asked FVAP staff to identify their divisions' inputs, activities, outputs, customers, and outcomes and consider how the proposed elements would support the proxy mission. Staff wrote down the inputs, activities, outputs, outcomes, partners, and customers on sheets of paper and taped them to a room-length white board under the appropriate category headings.[4] The success of the workshop depended not on whether it yielded a "pretty picture" but on whether the staff walked away with a clearer understanding of the relationships among the things they do as an institution and why they do them.

We took gleanings from the workshop and used them to create a rough mockup of the benchmark model. Construction of the model was an iterative process. We met with members of the FVAP staff, primarily in small groups, to obtain feedback on elements of the model and, eventually, on the model in its totality. We met with FVAP to discuss the model, we revised the model, we met with FVAP again, and so forth. The model was complete when participants reached agreement on the content and structure.

The development of the benchmark model (see Figure 2.2 in Chapter Two) was an act of synthesis. It was based largely on FVAP's sense of itself, as conveyed both orally, through the workshop and discussions with staff, and in writing, through strategic documents. Thus, it represented the agency's "theory" of its operations, absent testing and validation. Moreover, it contained considerable detail because, as a matter of process, FVAP leadership and staff needed to be able to "find themselves" in the model, which sometimes required that we call out specific tasks and work products with concrete examples. The modeling exercise helped us, the RAND team, and FVAP to see how the parts might—or might not—fit together as a whole.

The benchmark logic model provided a diagnostic tool for surfacing issues that merited closer consideration and, thus, informed the next steps in the project. It raised questions about FVAP's coherence as an agency, the strength and value of its connections to stakeholders, and the nature of outcomes. It also confirmed the blurriness of FVAP's mission and suggested holes in our understanding of both the agency and its role in the voting community.

Test, Validate, and Refine the Logic Model

In the next step of the process, we reached out to FVAP's partners and other intermediaries, and we looked more closely at FVAP's legal requirements to test, validate, and refine the model—that is, to determine whether the model, as developed through our work with FVAP and largely reflective of the agency's perspective, was accurate. It was possible that we had missed or mischaracterized elements of the model or the path from

---

[4] Greenfield, Shelton, et al., 2015, includes a photograph of the results.

inputs to outcomes. The logic model provided us with a point of departure for identifying particular stakeholders of interest, including election officials; overseas-citizen groups; voting assistance personnel in the Air Force, Army, Navy, Marine Corps, Coast Guard, and Department of State; congressional staff; and academics and technologists. We also looked at the legislation on voting assistance to pinpoint the minimum set of activities that FVAP must undertake to satisfy specific, direct requirements, to which we referred as "core" requirements; to improve our understanding of how FVAP's activities related to those requirements; and to ensure that we were appropriately capturing those requirements in the model, to the extent that the agency was meeting them.[5] Thus, we were able to test and validate what we believed we already understood about the agency—as depicted in the benchmark logic model—and explore the strength and value of the stakeholder interface.

Identify Gaps and Disconnects

Whereas the benchmark logic model flowed from our discussions with FVAP and thus represented the "FVAP-centric" perspective, the stakeholder engagement and requirement assessment allowed us to see FVAP as others saw it. When we compared these perspectives, we found evidence of gaps and disconnects, not just in how we had represented FVAP in the benchmark logic model but also in the agency's program design and implementation. Whereas the previous step had us looking for inaccuracies in our depiction of the model, this step had us looking for organizational challenges. Would the model work to achieve intended outcomes, and would it accomplish everything that it needed to accomplish? The analysis strongly suggested that FVAP, its stakeholders, and the law were seeing the world differently and that some of those differences were, in fact, suggestive of challenges. We uncovered significant differences between FVAP's perceptions of itself, as embodied in the benchmark logic model, and the stakeholders' perceptions of FVAP. For example, FVAP saw itself as operating through intermediaries, but those same intermediaries, including some of the uniformed-service representatives, election officials, and overseas NGO staff with whom we spoke, did not see a clear path from FVAP's research-related, training, and other program activities to them or to UOCAVA voters. The assessment of legal and policy requirements did not reveal any chasms, but it suggested room for realignment within and among FVAP's activities.

---

[5]   In this step, we looked to U.S. law on UOCAVA voting and U.S. Department of Defense (DoD) policy, to draw distinctions among those activities that are mandated in law, those that are called for in DoD policy, and those that FVAP has some latitude to alter based on institutional priorities and resource availability; however, as we explain in Greenfield, Shelton, et al., 2015, we chose to focus more on law than on policy.

Provide Initial Recommendations and Guidance on Realignment

We recast the findings as actionable recommendations for improving the agency's strategic focus and strengthening its operations and organizational structure and provided initial guidance for implementing change. By the time we delivered the recommendations and guidance formally, FVAP had begun to act on most of them. This was possible, in part, because we shared findings as they emerged, to generate debate and discussion and facilitate change. In a series of meetings with FVAP leadership and staff, we suggested that FVAP begin by solidifying its mission and resolving issues of purpose and priorities, an effort on which it had already embarked in the months preceding our engagement, and expand its efforts from there to build stronger relationships with its stakeholders and act more effectively.

Probe Gaps and Disconnects

The preceding analysis of FVAP's strategy and operations established the need and laid the groundwork for a better understanding of FVAP's engagement with its operating environment and deeper consideration of its ability to support that engagement analytically. In the next phase of the project, we continued to explore the points of connectivity in the logic model—the real and virtual interfaces between FVAP and its stakeholders—but we did so using a broader analytical lens, i.e., one of a larger voting assistance system.[6]

We considered the agency's engagement within the system in two ways, both of which were important to FVAP and its stakeholders and appeared to merit further attention on the basis of our preliminary assessments in earlier steps of the project.

First, we considered FVAP's approach to managing and disseminating findings from research. FVAP appeared to lack analytical capabilities and capacities, some of which could be filled through professional development, and a method for selecting projects and carrying them out effectively. To address the methodological gap, we began developing a checklist and worksheet for project selection and management, based largely on existing frameworks and informed by principles of benefit–cost assessment and risk assessment.[7] As that work progressed, we found that the checklist and worksheet could serve more-general purposes. FVAP could use these materials to manage a broad range of projects and activities, including some that do not relate to research.

Second, we considered FVAP's engagement with Voting Assistance Officers (VAOs) and Installation Voter Assistance (IVA) offices, which serve as conduits of

---

[6] We use the term *system* to refer to the various providers of voting assistance to UOCAVA voters and the ways in which they relate to each other—as a loosely formed network, rather than a formal system.

[7] Greenfield, Shelton, et al., 2015, Appendix D, presents and discusses the checklist and worksheet.

voting assistance from FVAP to UOCAVA voters. We focused on FVAP's work with military installations, including the IVA offices, and applied the newly developed checklist and worksheet to draw lessons for strengthening the VAO training program, which FVAP operates.[8]

This analysis largely confirmed the gaps and disconnects that we uncovered earlier (e.g., that FVAP was heavily reliant on others but was not necessarily engaging with them well), but it also improved our understanding of both the rules at play and the "ground truth" and their implications for the contours and conduct of voting assistance. We found that the voting assistance system consists of many potential providers of voting assistance and points of service (military and civilian, physical or virtual) to which UOCAVA voters can turn for help in the voting process (Figure 3.2) and that FVAP plays an important, but not all-inclusive, part in successful voting. This depiction improved FVAP's understanding of the institutional relationships that are required to deliver assistance to UOCAVA voters. Of particular interest is the fact that the system-wide perspective drew further attention to the importance of stakeholder engagement and enabled us to identify specific ways in which FVAP could better leverage its position in the system through elements of the VAO training program.

Provide Additional Recommendations and Guidance on Realignment

Building on the initial recommendations and guidance and the further exploration of FVAP's research-related and military installation–based activities, we provided FVAP with additional recommendations and guidance in each of those areas and worked with FVAP on the development and refinement of the final, robust logic model (Figure 3.3). The robust logic model, which represented the "should-be" version of FVAP, informed FVAP's decisions about organizational and operational changes. Because we worked closely with FVAP throughout the project, it began to implement change early in the project, and, by the time the project reached its conclusion, the agency had already taken on some or many features of the model. In that way, the "should be" and the "as is" began to converge.

Among the most-noteworthy features of the robust logic model was the reformulation of voter assistance to include all conduits of assistance to voters, including the uniformed services, election officials, NGOs, and direct to voters, and the technology that undergirds that assistance. Thus, both the voter assistance and election-official assistance activity streams and the technological component of institutional support that appeared previously in the benchmark model now appear under a single heading—namely, the newly expanded category of voter assistance. That change made

---

[8] FVAP provides training on UOCAVA voting assistance to VAOs, unit VAOs, IVA office staff, State Department representatives, and election officials. Here, we use the term *VAO training* to encompass all military installation– and embassy-based training other than that provided directly to UOCAVA voters.

Figure 3.2
Voting Assistance Opportunities and Paths to Success for Uniformed and Overseas Citizens Absentee Voting Act Voters

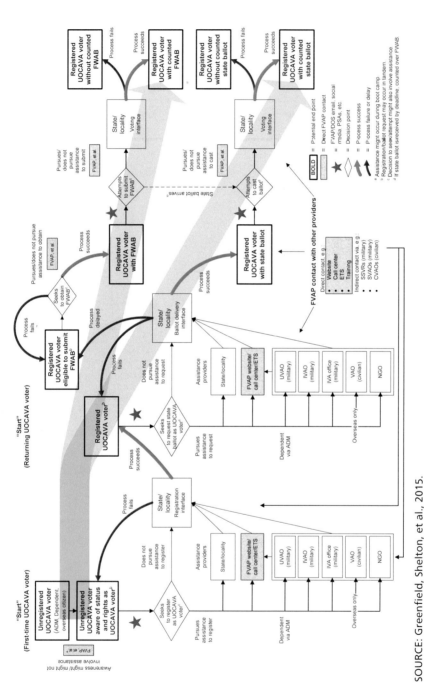

SOURCE: Greenfield, Shelton, et al., 2015.
NOTE: ADM = active-duty military. ETS = Electronic Transmission Service. UVAO = unit VAO. IVAO = installation VAO. FWAB = Federal Write-In Absentee Ballot. SSVR = Senior Service Voting Representative. SVAO = Service Voting Action Officer. CVAO = chief VAO.

RAND RR882/1-3.2

Figure 3.3
Federal Voting Assistance Program Robust Logic Model

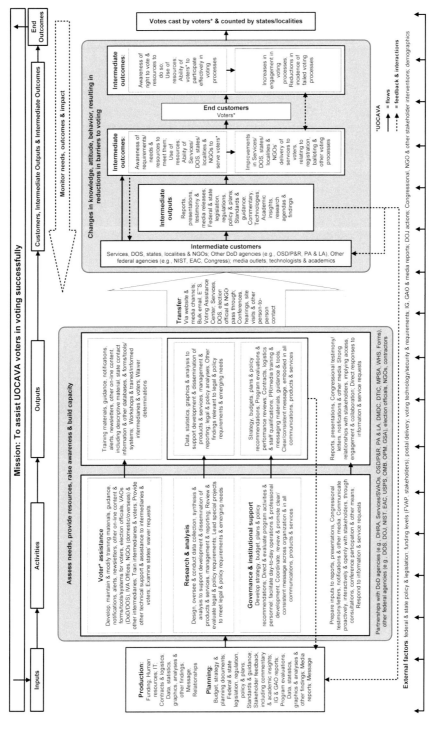

SOURCE: Greenfield, Shelton, et al., 2015.

RAND RR882/1-3.3

it possible to eliminate much of the repetition that we observed in the benchmark model, to streamline the agency's activities and outputs, and to streamline our presentation of intermediate customers. It was no longer necessary to assign customers to particular activity streams; rather, the model recognized the agency's customers as relating to the agency as a whole, suggesting greater institutional coherence and recognizing the agency's overarching intent as encapsulated in the still-valid summary mission statement.[9]

At the same time, the model also draws together all of FVAP's data collection and other research-related activities in a single unit labeled "research and analysis." The separate heading gives prominence to the agency's research-related functions that were previously buried under "technical services" and obliquely conceptualized.[10]

Another difference in the robust model was its comparative generality. Whereas the benchmark model was full of specific examples of guidance, media, tools, data, statistics, and special projects, this version has few or none. It was necessary to include those details in the benchmark model, first, so that FVAP and we could see the agency in its entirety and, second, to substitute for a shared vocabulary for describing its operations. FVAP leadership and staff needed to be able to locate themselves in the model; without the examples, we could not be certain at that stage in the project that everyone was using such words as *guidance, media,* or *tools* in the same way or that FVAP's leadership and staff shared a common understanding of the organization. With a fuller understanding of the agency and a shared vocabulary, both of which came to fruition over the course of the project, users of the model did not require as many details. FVAP staff and leadership could see themselves in the model, were using vocabulary consistently, and could describe and explain their roles to others, even without the detail.

In addition, the rearticulated model covers all the core requirements that we identified in the assessment of FVAP's legal requirements. If FVAP were to follow this model, it would have some assurance that it was undertaking the activities necessary to meet those requirements.

Gather Evidence of Change and Realignment

Over the course of the project—both in response to our analysis and through the organization's own initiatives—FVAP began to change. In the final step of our analysis, we explored the extent of this change as manifest in tangible evidence. For example, we reviewed the layout and content of the FVAP website, which FVAP had redesigned

---

[9]   See the related discussion under "Gather Evidence of Change and Realignment."

[10]   The framing of "technical services" in the benchmark logic model was reflective more of the role of these activities in the organization in the earliest stages of the project than of their position in the agency's organization chart, which was quite prominent at that time.

and repopulated; compared its latest organization chart (Figure 3.4) to its earlier rendition (Figure 2.3 in Chapter Two); gathered information about the agency's recent work with stakeholders through the Council of State Governments (CSG) and in other venues; looked over information on the usage of the voting assistance center and customer satisfaction; obtained a summary of FVAP's professional development activities and plans; and reached out to some of FVAP's stakeholders in the uniformed services to get their perspectives on changes within the agency.

We found some of the clearest examples of change in the redesign of FVAP's website, FVAP's new statement of purpose, and FVAP's reorganization. For a detailed discussion of the changes in the website, including before and after snapshots, and other areas of the agency's management and operations, please see Greenfield, Shelton, et al., 2015. Here, we focus on the agency's statement of purpose and organizational structure.

The logic-modeling process not only shed light on the ambiguity of the agency's understanding and articulation of its mission but also fueled internal deliberations that led to the new statement. In broad terms, the general representation of the agency's mission, "to assist UOCAVA voters in voting successfully," remained applicable, albeit better understood, and continued to serve as a summary statement in the final, robust logic model. However, the new statement adds clarity to the meaning and scope of assistance, by referencing voter awareness, tools and resources for voting, and global accessibility.

The agency's new organizational configuration (Figure 3.4) largely parallels the configuration of the final, robust logic model, which provided a blueprint for FVAP's reorganization. The robust model depicted all voter assistance, whether channeled through military installations, election officials, or NGOs, in a single stream, which parallels the agency placing all such activities in a single division.

We assessed all of the changes in relation to our earlier recommendations about FVAP's mission and organization, stakeholder relationships, and effectiveness. (See Appendix B for a summary of the evidence in relation to those recommendations.) In some cases, we found evidence of outright change, such as the agency's redesign of its website. In other instances, we found evidence of progress being made, such as enrollment in professional development programs. And in yet other cases, we found evidence of unevenness, suggesting that, although the agency had moved forward in many respects, work remained to be done.

Provide Final Recommendations and Guidance for Realignment

Although there was evidence of positive change at FVAP, we saw the potential for both additional gains and fatigue. As a result, our final recommendations and guidance to FVAP focused on how to lock in and build on recent progress. We recommended that

Figure 3.4
Federal Voting Assistance Program Organization Chart as of February 2015

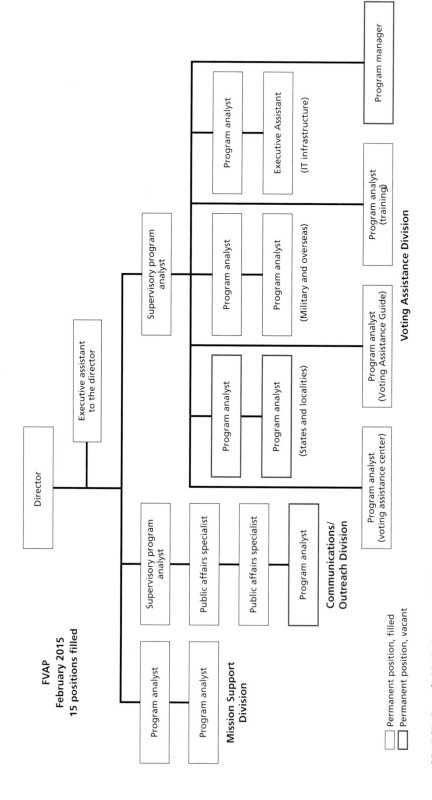

SOURCE: Greenfield, Shelton, et al., 2015.
NOTE: FVAP provided updated information in February 2015, which we included in this figure.
RAND RR882/1-3.4

FVAP adhere to its mission, notwithstanding the near certainty of some leadership turnover, the push and pull of divergent stakeholder interests, and the ebbs and flows of election cycles. At the same time, FVAP must be able to respond to emerging needs, some foreseeable and some not. To consolidate and advance recent progress, FVAP would need to continue working on unifying the organization, improving its relationships with stakeholders, and embracing effectiveness. Some of our specific suggestions[11] were within FVAP's power to implement, and others needed to be taken up elsewhere in DoD, at higher organizational levels, or outside DoD.

Summary of the Process

The FVAP project was structured as a long-term logic-modeling effort as depicted in Figure 3.1. The following process steps that we used with FVAP can be applied to other programs or agencies with similar concerns about their strategic and operational alignment:

- Learn about the agency's mission, strategy, and operations from the agency's perspective, and document the findings in a logic model.
- Use the benchmark model to develop a clearer understanding of the relationships between the agency's activities and the reasons for those activities.
- Apply the logic model as a diagnostic tool to identify issues that merit closer attention, and shape the next steps of the modeling project.
- Gather external perspectives of the agency to test and validate the logic model, identify inaccuracies, and make refinements.
- Compare internal and external perspectives to identify gaps and disconnects in the program's design and implementation.
- Create actionable recommendations for improving the agency's strategic focus and strengthening its operations and organizational structure, and provide initial guidance for implementing change.
- Explore points of connectivity between FVAP and it stakeholders by, for example, using the broader analytic lens of the system in which the agency operates.
- Develop a robust logic model to inform decisions about strategic and operational changes, including changes in the design of the organization.
- Explore the extent to which the agency changed based on tangible evidence.
- Create final recommendations focused on how to lock in and build on progress.

---

[11] See Chapter Eight of Greenfield, Shelton, et al., 2015.

CHAPTER FOUR

Concluding Remarks

In broad terms, the logic-modeling approach served its purpose. We delivered recommendations and implementing guidance to provide FVAP with the means to more effectively focus its strategy, organize and execute its operations, and interact with its stakeholders to serve its mission. FVAP, for its part, worked with us to inform the process and suggest tactical changes in the approach and used interim findings to formulate and expedite institutional change.

Outcomes of the Collaboration

We cannot, as yet, connect FVAP's reorientation and reorganization to improvements in outcomes for UOCAVA voters—the changes in FVAP are too recent and largely untested—but the steps that FVAP has taken to realign its strategy and operations by refocusing its program design and implementation should cut a clearer path from the program's activities to outcomes and, thus, better support those outcomes. Looking to the future, the logic model can assist in gauging progress, as a basis for deriving metrics and measures with which to assess the agency's performance. In that way, the logic model can contribute to future "health checks" that might enable the agency to stay on track.

In a related RAND project, FVAP commissioned the development of a dashboard to provide indicators of needs throughout the voting assistance system and track progress toward meeting those needs. Moreover, with input from that project, FVAP has redesigned its VAO and IVA office metric reporting requirements. The new requirements include an updated list of metrics and the justification for each metric.

Observations

We conclude by offering observations on the relative merits of taking a highly collaborative approach as compared with a more hands-off approach and commenting on some of the crucial elements of the collaboration.

The benefits of a highly collaborative logic-modeling approach are that the approach is more likely to meet the organization's needs, engender buy-in from leadership and staff, and result in sustainable change. Recent studies of change management support this claim (e.g., Aiken and Keller, 2009). Moreover, we note that FVAP, in particular, felt that it needed something other than an arm's-length engagement.

The costs of the highly collaborative logic-modeling approach are resource requirements, the risks of early action, and the potential for cooption. First, the approach used required a high degree of managerial focus and staff involvement. Our engagement with FVAP required substantial FVAP staff involvement, including meetings at all levels of the organization and in groups ranging in size from few to many. Second, by offering preliminary guidance and recommendations from an incomplete analysis, we risked the possibility that early action based on erroneous conclusions would make things worse instead of better. To mitigate that risk, we bracketed early findings in our conversations with FVAP and suggested holding off on instituting changes in those areas that clearly required additional probing, such as research and training. Third, in a closely collaborative relationship, the potential for cooption merits consideration. For that reason, we strongly recommend incorporating external inputs, including stakeholder perspectives, and triangulating across sources of information about the agency.

We see the successful implementation of the collaborative logic-modeling approach as demonstrating to FVAP, to other DoD agencies, and to other governmental and nongovernmental agencies that they can take concrete action to overcome obstacles to change and place themselves among the minority of organizations that implements change successfully. As both experience and the large literature on change management suggest, organizational change is difficult but still attainable. The collaboration between RAND and FVAP began before the start of the project with an intense period of discussion around the terms of the engagement. The project launched with an inclusive and expansive attempt to better understand the organization from its perspective, from the perspective of its stakeholders, and from the perspective of the laws and policies governing it. We employed a standard, time-tested, and readily available method—namely, logic modeling—which we supplemented with stakeholder outreach, a requirement assessment, and consideration of the larger voting assistance system. And the collaborative relationship made it possible for FVAP to make changes expeditiously. Two human factors also stood out as essential to progress: the agency's commitment to implementing change from the outset and the mutual trust that an ongoing, collaborative relationship can engender.

Logic-Modeling Workshop Materials

In this appendix, we present the logic-modeling references and resources, agenda, and discussion points that we (the RAND project team) prepared for FVAP for the workshop that we led on May 1–2, 2013.[1] The materials have been modified slightly to better match the style of this report.

In addition to these materials, we also provided FVAP with a short primer on logic modeling that we reproduced, in large part, in Chapter Two of this report. We designed the primer as a "leave behind" to accompany our presentation on logic modeling, "Logic Modeling 101," which was the first full session of the logic-modeling workshop.

References and Resources for the Logic-Modeling Workshop

Greenfield, Victoria A., Valerie L. Williams, and Elisa Eiseman, *Using Logic Models for Strategic Planning and Evaluation: Application to the National Center for Injury Prevention and Control*, Santa Monica, Calif.: RAND Corporation, TR-370-NCIPC, 2006. As of July 21, 2015: http://www.rand.org/pubs/technical_reports/TR370.html

Greenfield, Victoria A., Henry H. Willis, and Tom LaTourrette, *Assessing the Benefits of U.S. Customs and Border Protection Regulatory Actions to Reduce Terrorism Risks*, Santa Monica, Calif.: RAND Corporation, CF-301-INDEC, 2012. As of July 21, 2015: http://www.rand.org/pubs/conf_proceedings/CF301.html

McLaughlin, John A., and Gretchen B. Jordan, "Logic Models: A Tool for Telling Your Program's Performance Story," *Evaluation and Program Planning*, Vol. 22, No. 1, February 1999, pp. 65–72.

Taylor-Powell, Ellen, and Ellen Henert, *Developing a Logic Model: Teaching and Training Guide*, Madison, Wis.: University of Wisconsin–Extension, Cooperative Extension, February 2008. As of July 21, 2015: http://www.uwex.edu/ces/pdande/evaluation/pdf/lmguidecomplete.pdf

Wholey, Joseph S., Harry P. Hatry, and Kathryn E. Newcomer, eds., *Handbook of Practical Program Evaluation*, 3rd ed., San Francisco, Calif.: Jossey-Bass, 2010.

---

[1]   We have added a small number of citations, references, and resources.

Williams, Valerie L., Elisa Eiseman, Eric Landree, and David M. Adamson, *Demonstrating and Communicating Research Impact: Preparing NIOSH Programs for External Review*, Santa Monica, Calif.: RAND Corporation, MG-809-NIOSH, 2009. As of July 21, 2015: http://www.rand.org/pubs/monographs/MG809.html

W. K. Kellogg Foundation, *Logic Model Development Guide*, Battle Creek, Mich., 2004.

Logic-Modeling Workshop Agenda

The following agenda was prepared for the logic-modeling workshop, held at FVAP, with FVAP staff, including leadership, on May 1–2, 2013. Although it is not reflected in the agenda, the second day concluded with a conversation about stakeholder perceptions.

May 1, 2013
Full Group Participation

1:30–1:35	Welcome (FVAP)
1:35–1:45	Objectives and expectations (RAND)
1:45–2:30	**Logic Modeling 101 (RAND-led)**
2:30–2:45	Q&A
2:45–3:00	Break
3:00–4:00	**Why Does FVAP Exist? (RAND-led)**
4:00–4:30	Day 2 Preview, including breakout group assignments

May 2, 2013
Consecutive Breakout Groups

8:30–9:25	Breakout group I Voting Assistance
9:30–10:25	Breakout group II Election Official Assistance
10:30–11:25	Breakout group III Technology
11:30–12:25	Breakout group IV Mission Support[2]

"Who," "what," and "why" (RAND-led)

- What inputs, activities, and outputs are associated with your program area?
- How do your outputs get used and by whom?
- What are the intended outcomes?
- What are the program area's boundaries?
- What types of external factors come into play?

12:30–1:00	Lunch

---

[2]   This group included the communication services group.

Full Group Participation

1:00–2:00	Reconvene, reflect, and discuss (RAND-led)
2:00–2:15	Break
2:15–3:45	Laying the foundation for FVAP's logic model together (RAND-led)
3:45–4:00	Recap and next steps (RAND and FVAP)

Discussion Points

The following discussion points (verbatim) were sent to FVAP as read-ahead material for the logic modeling workshop, held on May 1–2, 2013.

Introduction

For the purposes of these discussion points, please think of FVAP as a "program," as the acronym implies, and your work as occurring in a "program area" within that program. That area, however you choose to define it, could correspond to an FVAP division, such as "election official assistance"; cut across divisions, as might be true in the case of legal affairs and policy; or constitute a subset of a division. These points, which are intended to foster discussion today and in the future, address three basic logic modeling concepts: (1) who are "you," as a program or program area; (2) what are "you" doing; and (3) why are "you" doing it? You might find that some of the points seem to repeat or overlap, but, sometimes, asking a question in different ways or from different perspectives can help generate a better discussion.

Program Area Definition

- How are you defining your program area?
- Where does it stand in relation to other FVAP program areas; that is, in what division or divisions does your program area reside and with which other divisions and/or program areas does it interact? How do your actions affect them; how do their actions affect you? Do you provide support to others within FVAP and do others provide support to you? If so, in what ways do you/they provide support?

Program/Program Area Mission and Goals

- What is your program/program area trying to achieve and why?
- Who are its primary customers, partners, and other stakeholders?
- How do you define them?

Program/Program Area Inputs

- What types of physical and institutional infrastructure support activities in your program area, e.g., IT systems, planning and funding processes . . . ?
- What other resources do you use to undertake or plan for activities, e.g., funding, staff, customer/partner/stakeholder feedback, survey data, legal authority, planning documents, DoD instructions . . . ?

Program/Program Area Activities

- What does your program/program area do, e.g., analyzes survey findings, develops training tools, awards grants, builds capacity, develops and/or validates new methods and technologies, assesses threats, responds to Congressional inquiries . . . ?
- Do you work with partners inside FVAP, inside DoD, outside DoD? If so, how, how often, and to what end? Are they central to your activities?

Program/Program Area Outputs

- What does your program/program area "produce," e.g., reports, data bases, methods, tools, technologies, training/education materials, workshops, pilot programs, demonstration projects, best practices, marketing/outreach materials, Congressional replies, other?

Dissemination and Transfer of Outputs

- How are the outputs of your program/program area disseminated or transferred to their intended audiences, e.g., do you post materials on website, provide email alerts, and/or convene meetings . . . ? Are strategies in place to ensure effective dissemination and transfer of your outputs? If so, what are they?
- What individuals, agencies, NGOs, businesses and/or other entities receive or request the outputs, both within and outside of FVAP, and what are their respective roles in the voting community? (Some outputs might be intended to meet the needs of intermediaries, who might, in turn, pass the outputs on to other stakeholders; other outputs might flow directly to ultimate beneficiaries, e.g., UOCAVA voters.) How significant are these individuals/entities in the voting community?

Outcomes and Program/Program Area Contribution

- How do these individuals, agencies, businesses, etc. use—or respond to—the outputs that flow from program/program area activities? Do they use the outputs in their current form, as produced, or do they modify them?
- In what ways might their use of program/program area outputs result in changes in knowledge, attitudes, and behavior? At what level are these changes expected to occur, e.g., individual, agency, NGO, business, etc.?
- What is the intended outcome of those changes?
- How will this chain of events—and your program/program area's contribution, in particular—help to fill a societal need or solve a societal problem?
- Who will benefit, ultimately?

Program/Program Area Responsibilities

- What are the program/program area's boundaries? How do its activities relate to those of your customers, partners, and other stakeholders?
- What is the program/program area's niche in the voting community?

External Factors

- What outside forces affect your use of inputs, your activities, the outputs of your activities, and the effects of your activities, e.g., legislative actions, changes in technology, changes in structures of other agencies . . . ?

APPENDIX B

Evidence of Change

Table B.1 presents evidence of change within FVAP in relation to a series of initial recommendations that we provided to FVAP.

Table B.1
Evidence of Change in Relation to Preliminary Recommendations and Guidance

General Recommendation	Areas of Emphasis	Evidence of Change
Become one FVAP	Come to terms with the mission	• Reorientation of the mission and purpose • Redesign of the FVAP website and its content and outreach and training materials • Reorganization of the agency • Reconfiguration of the call center as an in-house voting assistance center • New forms of engagement with states, potentially including ongoing work with CSG • Reassessment of DoD Instruction 1000.04
	Integrate and shore up operations	• Reorganization of the agency • Reconfiguration of the call center as an in-house voting assistance center and related cross-training of FVAP staff • Enrollment in professional development programs, including training in human resources and organizational management
	Sharpen and clarify the message	• Reorientation of the mission and purpose • Redesign of the FVAP website and its content and outreach and training materials

Table B.1—Continued

General Recommendation	Areas of Emphasis	Evidence of Change
Build trust and strengthen relationships	Work with partners and serve customers	• Redesign of the FVAP website and its content and outreach and training materials • Reconfiguration of the call center as an in-house voting assistance center • New forms of engagement with states, potentially including ongoing work with CSG • Outreach to DoD Education Activity schools • National Association of Secretaries of State resolution on voting information • Continuation of OMB process for form (FPCA and FWAB) revisions
	Communicate better and more regularly	• Redesign of the FVAP website and its content and outreach and training materials • Customer feedback on voting assistance center operations • New forms of engagement with states, potentially including ongoing work with CSG • Enrollment in professional development programs, including training in customer service skills and techniques
	Operate as openly as possible	• New forms of engagement with states, potentially including ongoing work with CSG • Continuation of OMB process for form (FPCA and FWAB) revisions • Development of research briefs
Embrace a culture and principles of effectiveness	Engage routinely in benefit–cost assessment or employ other analytical methods	• Use of findings from the 2012 postelection report to Congress (FVAP, 2013) • Development of a dashboard[a] • Enrollment in professional development programs, including training in organizational and project management, strategic planning and tactical execution, performance measurement, and problem-solving and data analysis • Staff interest in use of project-management tools

SOURCE: Greenfield, Shelton, et al., 2015.

NOTE: FPCA = Federal Post Card Application.

[a] The availability of metrics—and other information—from the voting assistance center suggests another potential avenue of change.

References

Aiken, Carolyn, and Scott Keller, "The Irrational Side of Change Management," *McKinsey Quarterly*, Vol. 2, No. 10, April 2009, pp. 100–109. As of December 17, 2015:
http://www.mckinsey.com/insights/organization/the_irrational_side_of_change_management

DoD Instruction 1000.04—*See* Under Secretary of Defense for Personnel and Readiness, 2012.

Federal Voting Assistance Program, *2012 Post-Election Report to Congress*, June 2013; referenced November 20, 2013. As of July 26, 2015:
http://www.fvap.gov/uploads/FVAP/Reports/2012report.pdf

FVAP—*See* Federal Voting Assistance Program.

Greenfield, Victoria A., Shoshana R. Shelton, Edward Balkovich, John S. Davis II, and David M. Adamson, *The Federal Voting Assistance Program and the Road Ahead: Achieving Institutional Change Through Analysis and Collaboration*, Santa Monica, Calif.: RAND Corporation, RR-882-OSD, 2015. As of November 9, 2011:
http://www.rand.org/pubs/research_reports/RR882.html

Greenfield, Victoria A., Valerie L. Williams, and Elisa Eiseman, *Using Logic Models for Strategic Planning and Evaluation: Application to the National Center for Injury Prevention and Control*, Santa Monica, Calif.: RAND Corporation, TR-370-NCIPC, 2006. As of July 21, 2015:
http://www.rand.org/pubs/technical_reports/TR370.html

Greenfield, Victoria A., Henry H. Willis, and Tom LaTourrette, *Assessing the Benefits of U.S. Customs and Border Protection Regulatory Actions to Reduce Terrorism Risks*, Santa Monica, Calif.: RAND Corporation, CF-301-INDEC, 2012. As of July 21, 2015:
http://www.rand.org/pubs/conf_proceedings/CF301.html

Landree, Eric, Hirokazu Miyake, and Victoria A. Greenfield, *Nanomaterial Safety in the Workplace: Pilot Project for Assessing the Impact of the NIOSH Nanotechnology Research Center*, Santa Monica, Calif.: RAND Corporation, RR-1108-NIOSH, 2015. As of December 17, 2015:
http://www.rand.org/pubs/research_reports/RR1108.html

McLaughlin, John A., and Gretchen B. Jordan, "Logic Models: A Tool for Telling Your Program's Performance Story," *Evaluation and Program Planning*, Vol. 22, No. 1, February 1999, pp. 65–72.

Public Law 99-410, Uniformed and Overseas Citizens Absentee Voting Act, August 28, 1986.

Public Law 111-84, National Defense Authorization Act for Fiscal Year 2010, Subtitle H, "Military Voting," the Military and Overseas Voter Empowerment Act, October 28, 2009. As of July 21, 2015:
http://www.gpo.gov/fdsys/pkg/PLAW-111publ84/content-detail.html

Taylor-Powell, Ellen, and Ellen Henert, *Developing a Logic Model: Teaching and Training Guide*, Madison, Wis.: University of Wisconsin–Extension, Cooperative Extension, February 2008. As of July 21, 2015:
http://www.uwex.edu/ces/pdande/evaluation/pdf/lmguidecomplete.pdf

Under Secretary of Defense for Personnel and Readiness, *Federal Voting Assistance Program (FVAP)*, Department of Defense Instruction 1000.04, September 13, 2012. As of July 21, 2015:
http://www.dtic.mil/whs/directives/corres/pdf/100004p.pdf

Wholey, Joseph S., Harry P. Hatry, and Kathryn E. Newcomer, eds., *Handbook of Practical Program Evaluation*, 3rd ed., San Francisco, Calif.: Jossey-Bass, 2010.

Williams, Valerie L., Elisa Eiseman, Eric Landree, and David M. Adamson, *Demonstrating and Communicating Research Impact: Preparing NIOSH Programs for External Review*, Santa Monica, Calif.: RAND Corporation, MG-809-NIOSH, 2009. As of July 21, 2015:
http://www.rand.org/pubs/monographs/MG809.html

W. K. Kellogg Foundation, *Logic Model Development Guide*, Battle Creek, Mich., 2004.